Rocky's Adventure

by
Katrina Syran

ILLUSTRATIONS·MARTINA SELWAY

The Muller family love all their pets, and I can assure you it's a very lively household .

In the middle of the picturesque village, Rolle, in Switzerland, a family with four children and four animals live together in an old beautiful townhouse.

But this is Rocky's story, their parrot, and I must tell you, this is a true story.

Blosom ready
for her supper

Rocky loves to dance
...hey Rocky
...hay Rocky

Cookie
always
ready to
play ball

Barney loves
to Jump in the
lake, to
swim

"Rocky really annoys me"; shouted Hecktor

"He always attacks me, he bit me in the ear again, MUM!"

"Let me take him" said Henri, twin brother of Hecktor. He put him back into his enormous cage.

"I feel sorry for him" said Henri,"let's take the big cage out on the balcony so that he can watch the other birds and be outside in the lovely weather"

Hecktor still in pain from Rocky's bite hesitantly agreed.

They both pushed the enormous cage out onto their big brother Oscar's balcony looking over lake Geneva a hot spring day.

"Look he is so happy now" said Henri, "let's leave him out here for the afternoon"

The twin boys smelled mum's delicious banana cake and ran down to the kitchen.

Eating their cake Hecktor turned to Henri worryingly; "I can't hear his screams anymore..."

Henri with a mouthful mumbled; "I'm sure he is just happy watching the other birds flying around", suddenly his mouth felt dry," maybe best to check..."

They both ran upstairs to the top floor of their old town house.

"Oh no the cage is empty, the little food door is open.." little blond Henri cried.

Just that moment Hecktor saw from the balcony on the lake path a little girl running towards a lady with a green female parrot on her shoulder, the little girl grabbed the parrots feathered taile. The female parrot screamed and flew off and Hecktor screamed " Rocky" as he was certain he saw Rocky coming to the female parrots rescue and seeing both of them flying off together.

"On no, what are we supposed to tell Oscar" cried little Henri," he will be so angry with me."

Little Henri adored his big brother Oscar and did not want to upset him.

"I never liked Rocky, said Hecktor," I won't miss his screaming, besides he has found a girlfriend. I'm sure he is so much happier out there than inside this stupid cage. We have our lovely black lab Cookie & fox red lab Barney and pussycat Blossom to look after, Oscar will soon forget everything about Rocky"

It was a sunny warm day when Rocky flew off far away from his family in Rolle.

He could hear in the background Hecktor and Henri calling him but with this pretty parrot next to him there was no way he was turning back. Freedom, finally he could taste pure freedom. His beautiful big wings spread in full over lake Geneva with his green parrot girlfriend gurgling next to him.

Rocky felt like a king on top of the mountains.

Lake Geneva is surrounded by the French, Swiss alps with some forest.

They flew towards the forest in direction of Lausanne. There they settled into a tree and ate some of it leaves. It was starting to get dark. At home in Rolle, mum, dad, Hecktor, Henri, Oscar and their sister Benedica was desperately calling « Rocky » along the lake path. Oscar was in tears and Hecktor felt incredibly guilty about wanting Rocky to leave.

Back in the forest Rocky and his girlfriend were fast asleep, exhausted from their adventure.

Next day Rocky flew down from the tree to look for some seeds for himself and his girlfriend along the forest path. Suddenly a big man came up to him and before he could react the big man had thrown his T-shirt over him and Rocky was captured.

He tried to struggle free but this big man knew parrots and Rocky had no chance of escaping his capture. Rocky was brought into a new home with a round little lady greeting him.

She looked kind and gave Rocky some seeds. Suddenly the big man was back with a big pair of scissors. Rocky felt seriously worried and scared and was starting to miss his home in Rolle.

The big man reached out for him and Rocky flew around the room screaming.

The big man and the little round lady left the room and after a while Rocky settled back on the chair and nearly fell asleep.

Before Rocky could react the big hand of the big man held him in a way parrot owners only know how to hold a parrot and Rocky saw the shine of the big scissors clipping his beautiful big wings. This didn't hurt Rocky but he knew he would not ever be able to fly so far.

Rocky was crying seeing his feathers hitting the floor making him realise he would never again taste the sweet taste of freedom.

Rocky felt more and more sad.

He even started to miss Hecktor who annoyed him the most.

The round lady still gave him lovely grains and the man with the big hands stroke and cuddled him lots and taught him new words like; tea, and let him drink his delicious english breakfast tea with milk, but Rocky still felt sad.

He loved his lively household in Rolle with the curly haired mum the dad, two dogs, pussycat Blossom and four children.

Rocky particularly missed the music and the dancing.

They would always dance with him and sing his name to the rhythm, "hey Rocky hey Rocky", he absolutely loved that. Rocky loved dancing.

One day Rocky suddenly saw that his feathers started to fall out. It was normal that once in a while one could fall but now two three four beautiful pink feathers would fall out every day.

The round lady and big man must also have noticed because they both gave Rocky even more attention, they even let him into their bedroom at night.

But Rocky still felt very sad.

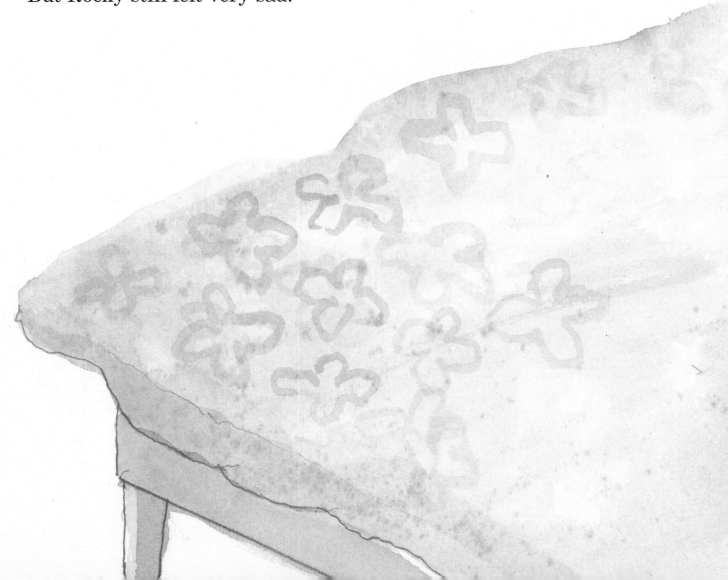

Then the man with the big hands put Rocky into a carton and into his truck.

Rocky felt excited!

Was the man going to bring him back to the forest?

Rocky prayed with all his little heart that the big man would take him back to his beautiful green girlfriend in the forest.

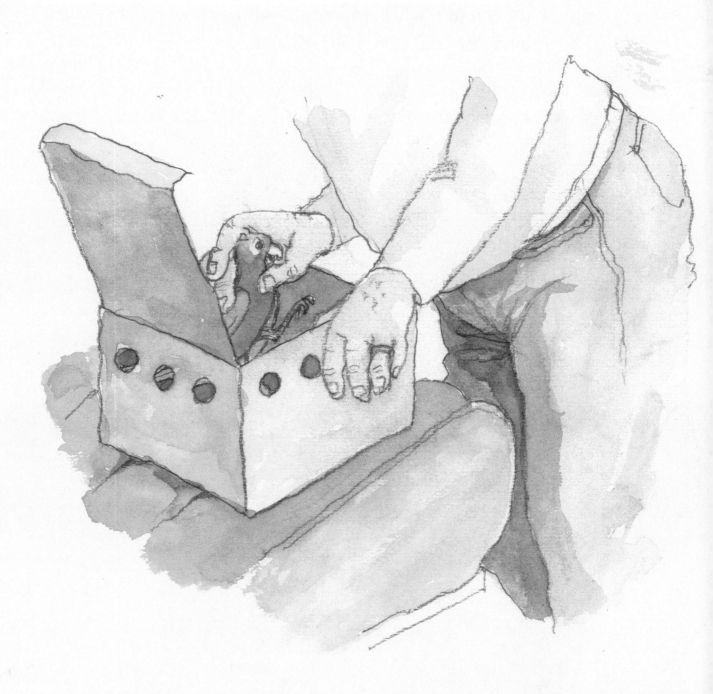

The truck stopped and the big man jumped out and got the carton. Rocky was carried into a big property in the middle of no where.

He could hear the sound of lots of different animals.

Dogs, cats, birds and many others unknown to him.

Rocky was wondering if the big man had brought him to a Zoo.

He could hear the big man speaking to another man and eventually that new man opened the carton and put Rocky into a bird cage.

He left the room.

Rocky was left alone and was starting to seriously worry what was going to happen next.

Meanwhile back in Rolle curly haired mum was shouting at everyone to get into the car.

She had just received a very exciting phone call with someone explaining that they believed Rocky was found.

Facebook has a lost and found page where Rocky had featured on for six months.

"Don't be too disappointed Oscar if it's not your parrot", mum said.

The twins held each others hands both praying it would really be Rocky. Hecktor had felt awful all this time and Henri often burst into tears thinking of Rocky. Especially now the last month when the weather had started to go colder.

Mum, dad, Benedica and the twins ran out of the car, Oscar walked slowly behind.

The same man who put Rocky in the cage came to greet them.

Rocky couldn't believe his eyes seeing his whole family standing in front of him and when mum started to sing "Hey Rocky", he danced and screamed with joy. He felt like the luckiest parrot on this planet and he promised himself never ever to leave his wonderful family ever again.

Archway Publishing books may be ordered through booksellers or by contacting:

Archway Publishing
1663 Liberty Drive
Bloomington, IN 47403
www.archwaypublishing.com
844-669-3957

Because of the dynamic nature of the Internet, any web addresses or links contained in this book may have changed since publication and may no longer be valid. The views expressed in this work are solely those of the author and do not necessarily reflect the views of the publisher, and the publisher hereby disclaims any responsibility for them.

Any people depicted in stock imagery provided by Getty Images are models, and such images are being used for illustrative purposes only. Certain stock imagery © Getty Images.

Interior Image Credit: Martina Selway

ISBN: 978-1-6657-0499-1 (sc)
ISBN: 978-1-6657-0500-4 (hc)
ISBN: 978-1-6657-0498-4 (e)

Print information available on the last page.

Archway Publishing rev. date: 06/23/2021

Printed in the United States
by Baker & Taylor Publisher Services